SPEAKING OF THE KINGDOM

*Published to mark the consecration of
Father Basil Osborne
as Bishop of Sergievo in
the Russian Orthodox Church
on 7th March 1993.*

Speaking of The Kingdom

The Coming of the Eighth Day

Bishop Basil Osborne

St Stephen's Press

Speaking of The Kingdom
© 1993 Basil Osborne

ALL RIGHTS RESERVED

ISBN 0-9519037-1-3

St Stephen's Press
30 Oxlease
Witney
Oxon OX8 6QX
United Kingdom
Tel & Fax 44.993.772834

Contents

Foreword 3

Dedication 8

The Way up is the Way down 9

Letting down the Net 12

Freedom in the Kingdom 15

"What have I to do with Thee, Jesus?" 19

No Escape from Incarnation 22

The Sabbath and the Eighth Day 26

To Give is to Receive 29

The Light of the World 34

We are Saved Together 38

Chief among Sinners? 41

Our Rest – God's Opportunity to Act 44

Preaching the Gospel to All Creation 49

Given Over to Death 55

The Power to Bind and to Loose 59

To Forgive is to Receive 63

In the Ship with Christ 67

Perfect as God is Perfect 71

"He Set His Face to Go to Jerusalem" 75

Good Works in a New Creation 77

Loosing the Bonds of Satan 80

Eternity – "God with us" 84

FOREWORD

There is a challenging poster that the Children's Society is currently using. It shows a young boy in some kind of trouble. The caption reads: "What I need is a good listening to." Those words turn on its head, in a parabolic way, the more common urge to administer "a good talking to". I remember in wayward and wilful moods as a child how resentful and rebellious I used to feel at the apparent one-sided unfairness of such a "talking to". It offended the keen childhood sense of justice. At school we used to call such speech acts "sermons" and with the arrogance of youth thought that gave us ample cause to disregard them.

Now the remarkable and paradoxical fact about Bishop Basil's sermons is that you end up feeling that you have been given a "good *listening* to" and you thereby find yourself inclined to regard them very seriously indeed. It is not the shifting clamorous ego that has been listened to. That surface self has been undermined because the hunger for love and truth in the depths of our being has been awakened and knows itself recognised and addressed. To listen and to be listened to become one in the Spirit. The hearers of his sermons always have a sense that Bishop Basil's own listening prevails over his speaking, so that what is said takes us all into the

Presence of the Eternal Listener, the Spirit in the midst.

Bishop Basil speaks quietly so that you see people stilling themselves, leaning forward to listen intently. For his form is concise and his style is sparingly austere, so you *have* to listen carefully. You also *want* to listen because his theology, his way of handling the Gospel passages and ideas and reflections on it, is stirring, often moving and nearly always with a note of extraordinary originality. How often we say to each other: "I don't know that I have ever heard that said quite like that before; I really need to read it and ruminate on it." So, here in this collection is our chance to do just that.

For me, his sermons open what we call in the Orthodox tradition "the place of the heart", where God and the human person meet. It is the place where we are called into being and action and know that we cannot respond and remain unchanged. The place of the heart is surely the Kingdom, both within and in our midst. In these sermons we experience the divine-human within and in our midst. In these sermons we experience the divine-human exchange of energies of the Kingdom at work – if only we will consent to participate: to love, to forgive, to seek the truth, to work for justice, to care for each other.

I sometimes feel as if I have previously been trying to look through a telescope with the focus blurred – one lens on the human situation, one on the call of the Divine, and me muddling along, somewhere, somehow. Occasionally through one of these sermons, the focus clicks sharply into place and I am left full of wonder and full too of at least a desire to act differently because of what I now see, hear, taste, smell, touch of the Way of the Kingdom. It evokes in me nostalgia, in the true sense of the word, a painful longing for home. Home is where we have not yet been. Home is the Kingdom which is and is to come.

To illustrate my points, I will confine myself to three sermons. I find myself pondering ever and again what Bishop Basil says about the Sacrament of Confession in the sermon, *To Forgive is To Receive*, on the debtor of Matt. 18: 23-25. "What God asks of us in confession is not that we should negotiate with him, but simply that we should acknowledge the existence of the debt and be then ready to do something about it... To receive the grace of forgiveness we do not need to ask for it. It is enough to acknowledge our debt. In fact, asking for forgiveness may even get in the way of clarity of mind and heart which is one of the primary goals of our practice of confession."

The sermon, *Preaching the Gospel to All Creation*, expresses the heart of an Orthodox ecology. It adds much to current ecumenical understanding because of the way it deals with the heights and depths of human and cosmic experience in relation to the Divine. It offers no easy romantic view but a deep joyful vision of the transfigured cosmos that has to carry within it potential tragedy which turns on our created freedom – that terrifying gift – to choose or refuse the coming of the Kingdom. With great skill Bishop Basil images the nexus of complex necessary truths about the interplay of the Divine and the human, all creation and all creatures. The sermon is about the divine-human ecology as well as that of nature and creatures. It is a real work of art, iconic, embodying itself in the image of the tender loving compassion for the body (nature, matter, the simply human) of the Myrrh-Bearing Women.

The sermon, *Given Over to Death*, comes from the time between the Ascension and Pentecost. My particular preoccupations as a psychotherapist make me very grateful for the way in which Bishop Basil witnesses to the experience of so many people who for some or much or most of life have to walk a "dark" path, where, however deep the essential faith, the felt experience will be of emptiness and the presence of God a paradoxical felt absence – an experience of death in life. Bishop Basil points out that we must remember "that it is by being 'given over to death' that our feet are placed on the path to eternal life." The depth of this kind of communion with God, as the sermon says, is not comfortable – and yet if borne can yield "a far more exceeding and eternal weight of glory".

Bishop Basil bears authentic witness to that hard path in Speaking of the Kingdom. Yet he never leaves us there. With true watchfulness and sobriety he reminds us too of the deep and mysterious truths of the Faith: Light which transfigures; Glory when suffering is borne; Resurrection after the cross. In the end – always God in Trinity and the transforming work of the God-Man and the life of the Holy Spirit in the Church across the ages, a tradition that it is our responsibility to hand on intact.

May these reflections on the Kingdom open all our hearts even more to the Presence of the Eternal Listener.

Wendy Robinson

Dedication

This collection is dedicated to the memory of Peter Novakovic and John Fennell, recently departed members of the Orthodox community at Oxford through whose support this publication has been made possible.

Eternal Remembrance!

THE WAY UP IS THE WAY DOWN

John 3: 13-17

Today is a very rich day for those who follow the Old or Julian Calendar. For not only are we celebrating the Resurrection of Christ, as we do each Sunday of the year, but with this Sunday there coincide both the Sunday before the Exaltation of the Cross and the feast of Joachim and Anna, the parents of the Mother of God and therefore the direct ancestors of Christ, the Incarnate God.

The Gospel passage I wish to draw your attention to this morning is, in fact, from the portion read in connection with the Exaltation of the Cross, the first verse of which reads: "No man hath ascended up to heaven, but he that came down from heaven, even the Son of man which is in heaven."

Christ is speaking here about Himself, and the primary thrust of the passage as a whole has to do with "lifting up", metaphorically a reference to His coming Crucifixion, though also to His ascension to sit at the right hand of the Father. But I wish to draw your attention this morning to His coming down, to the *descent* of Christ, not to the ascent. Because this, too, is something central to our faith, and something whose implication we do not always take on board. The Christian faith proclaims that the transcendent

God, existing from all eternity, from before the creation of the world, has descended, has come down into this world of space and time to become one of us, to become man, a human being: to become God *with us*, "Emmanuel". But He has also descended to reveal Himself as God *for* us, leaving heaven behind, so to speak, in order to give us the possibility of sharing His eternal life, of joining Him where *He* is.

It is this element of *descent*, which precedes any ascent, that I wish to stress. This descent is required for the transmission of life, and if we are to be Christ-like, if we are to be imitators of Christ , that descent must figure in our lives as well. Specifically, it is very easy to speak to those who live the same kind of spiritual life as we do: we understand one another, we speak the same language. What is difficult is to *descend*, to reach down to someone whose inner life is weak, or virtually non-existent. Yet, it is this ability that characterizes the saints. How many stories there are of St Seraphim, of St Tikhon of Zadonsk, which show their ability to descend from the high rung on which they stand to find the person before them, standing on a much lower rung, and gently draw him upward. In doing this they repeat, in their own way, the descent and ascent of Christ.

It is not difficult to reach those who want God: they will readily attend lectures and meetings, eager to know more about what already attracts them. But it is very difficult indeed to reach those whom *God* wants – and who may very well not want *Him*. Each of us should relate to his or her own life the descent of God into the world – God reaching down, in Christ, into a hostile or at the least indifferent world. And we should ask ourselves what we are doing that in any way reflects this saving action of God.

And we should apply the same standard to ourselves as a community. Are we reaching out to those whom God wants, or do we content ourselves with speaking politely to those who are already seeking God? Orthodoxy will never be truly established in this country, will never have fulfilled its mission, until it can speak directly and effectively to those who do not know – and do not care – that it – or God – exists. Amen.

22nd September 1991

LETTING DOWN THE NET

Luke 5: 1-11

The Gospel passage which we have heard this morning is one which we can hardly hear often enough, with its call to take up our cross to follow Christ. It is an example of what one might call the "Johannine" overtones of the Gospel of Luke. Luke has combined here two incidents which are found separated in Matthew and Mark: the account of Jesus teaching from a little ship moored off shore, and the miraculous draught of fishes, so great that it broke the net. And he has done so because, in his eyes, one incident comments on the other.

How they are related is only clear, however, if we consider just what is involved in fishing with a stationary net, which is what the Apostles were doing. This style of fishing involves simply letting down your net, spreading it out a bit and waiting. There is really nothing more you *can* do. You must prepare properly; you must see that your net does not have holes in it; you must use your skill and experience to choose the place where you will fish and manoeuvre your boat there without scaring off your prey. You should let down your net gently. But once the net is in place, you can do little more than wait: whether the fish swim into the net and are caught there is not up to you. Another power is involved.

Now it is this aspect of fishing which makes the story of the miraculous draft of fish into a comment on Christ's teaching from the boat off shore. In teaching, too, the most you can do is to prepare: master your material; think about how to present it; try not to scare off your audience. But once you have spoken, once the word has been uttered, the matter is no longer really in the teacher's hands: what happens next is in the hands of the students, helped of course in their efforts by the hand of God.

Christ himself uses the image of the sower to describe this process, as does St Paul: "I have planted, Apollos watered, but God gave the increase." (1 Cor. 3:6) In the parable of the sower, too, the harvest is dependent upon circumstances which are beyond the sower's control.

So it is in today's Gospel. For Luke, teaching is to some extent like fishing, and so he has put these two incidents together in his narrative. What is "Johannine" about this is that the miracle of the draught of fish speaks of more than obedience to Christ as master of the physical world. It is a revelation of the power of the spoken word when the reception of that word is prompted by the power and the grace of God.

Now all this is interesting – and, I hope, true. But the point I really wish to make is that today's Gospel has reference to us all. It is not only that we, too, can often say with the disciples: "Master, we have toiled all the night, and have taken nothing." The Gospel also says to *us* what Christ says to His disciples: "Do what I tell you to do, and I will take care of the rest."

The disciples act without knowing beforehand what the result will be, and in this way they show themselves to be worthy disciples of Christ. We, too, must often follow Christ without knowing what this will mean, without knowing what the result will be . And today's Gospel tells us that this is the way it *should* be: we may cast the net, but God provides what is caught; we may sow, others water, but God gives the increase. And we can act in the knowledge that if there were no increase, if we were to catch no fish, then that, too, is not without its relationship to our salvation.

So let us embrace the freedom which this understanding gives. Let us be content to be followers of Christ, and leave the outcome to Him. Amen

29th September 1991

FREEDOM IN THE KINGDOM

Luke 6: 31-36

Today's Gospel which is taken from St Luke's "Sermon on the Plain", is about freedom. This is true even if the word "freedom" itself never occurs in it. And to show this, I would like to go through this short passage verse by verse.

To begin with, Christ says, "As you would that men should do to you, do you also to them likewise." Here is the "Golden Rule": we are asked not to base our actions on what others *actually* do to us but to let our actions spring entirely from within, to let them be based on what we would *wish* them to do to us. We are invited to *act*, and not to *re*-act. What is more, we are told to act not on the basis of the past, of what *has* been, to leave aside even the question of what *should* be, and to open our action to the possibilities of the Kingdom, to the unbounded possibilities of the Age to Come, which flow from our hearts.

In the next verse Christ "shifts gear", so to speak, and now questions His audience – and us. What is so marvellous, He asks, about loving those who love us? We ourselves might ask: "Why is Christ here apparently criticising love?" Is not *all* love something marvellous, something that should be encouraged and praised? But Christ is not criticising love. He is pointing out that there is a conditional love, a love that is somehow dependent upon another, previously existing love, and to that extent is not truly free, does not have its origins within us, but is somehow elicited by what is without.

What Christ means is made even clearer in the two verses which follow, which deal with doing good to those who do good to us and lending where we can expect to receive something in return. In both cases, we are told, "sinners do the same." So what thanks have we?

But the real objection here is again that these actions are conditioned, one by the past, in that we do good because good has already been done to us; and one by the future, in that our lending is determined by our expectation of what *will* happen. In neither case are we truly free.

No, Christ says, to be free as I am free is to love where you are not loved, to do good where no good has been done to you, and to lend where you can hope for no reward. Do this, and you will be children – literally, *sons* – of the Most High. In more theological terms, do this, and you will demonstrate that what *I* am by nature, *you* have become by grace: sons, children of God. For God is kind to the thankless and the wicked; He is kind where kindness would not seem to be called for, and where it can expect no reward. Which is as much as to say that God is truly free, and invites us to be free with Him.

All this is then summed up in the final verse of today's reading: "Be ye merciful, as your Father also is merciful." To show mercy is to show gratuitous love, to show love where nothing calls for it and where no worldly calculation could lead us to expect a reward.

The greatest miracle of creation is not be found in the spectacular beauty, variety and power of nature, but in the fact that God has brought *freedom* out of nothingness. It is a freedom which He alone enjoyed before the world began, and to which He has now brought us. It is a freedom which is itself so great that it can only by fulfilled by grace. To become children of God, to become sons of God with the only Son of God, we need the Spirit of God dwelling within us, the Spirit whose presence enables Christ to dwell within us as well.

All of us will have some understanding of what this freedom means, of what it makes possible in our lives – and in the world. The challenge is to live in such a way that this understanding grows. Knowledge of this kind is itself a gift of the Spirit, and where the Spirit of God is present, there too is the power of God which enables us to act. May we use what we have been given to break into the deadening, often lethal, chain of cause and effect, which surrounds us as individuals and often seems to bind whole nations to the future and to the past. And may the freedom which is ours in Christ be a door for us, opening out into the Kingdom and eternal Life. Amen.

13th October 1991

"WHAT HAVE I TO DO WITH THEE, JESUS?"

Luke 8: 26-39

There are many striking aspects to today's Gospel reading about the Gadarene swine, but there are just two that I wish to draw to your attention. The first is what was said by the madman who met Jesus as He was getting out of the boat: "What have I to do with Thee, Jesus, Thou Son of God most high?"

Now this is *the* fundamental question, the question that each one of us must ask him or herself again and again. It is not as if baptism and membership of the Church bring an end to this question. It is not as if attendance at the Liturgy, or even receiving communion regularly make it unnecessary to repeat these words, applying them to ourselves. Nothing we ever do will make this question irrelevant. In no situation in which we find ourselves will they ever lose their power to bring us up short, to focus our minds and hearts on 'the one thing needful', to put us once again at the feet of Christ.

For those who have had a glimpse of what Jesus is, *who* Jesus is, the question of what we have to do with Him – and what He has to do with us – should remain, when not at the surface of our consciousness, then just beneath it. Because in Jesus, the "Son of God Most High", God Himself has come to us. And has done so as man, as a human being, as one of us. Nothing could be more important to us: the two poles of our reality, the human and the divine, brought together in one person, and He then presents Himself to us.

What is hard to understand – and at the same time, so sad – is that this makes so little difference in our lives. God comes to us, and we remain the same. Nothing illustrates more clearly the difficulty of the task God has set Himself – to create out of nothingness companions worthy of Himself. We receive Christ, and are unchanged. We are not even "tormented" by Christ, although the madman in the Gospel knows that Christ could torment *him*.. No. We are strangely unmoved. And in our unmovedness there is an implicit answer to the question, "What have I to with Thee?" And that answer is: "Little or nothing, I am afraid."

But the second feature of today's Gospel which I wish to draw to your attention is this: in it Jesus confronts the *madness* of this world, He meets it head on. And not only that – He enters it. And in that madness He finds recognition of Himself, and therefore the possibility of salvation. How important this is for all of us. Because the madman whom Christ confronts is not just someone who is clinically insane. He is the madman who has a place in the life of each of us. We all live to some extent in a world which is unreal, whether we have been driven there, or somehow entered it voluntarily. And Christ can meet us there, just as He met the man in today's Gospel.

We should all take heart from this. Christ comes to meet us where we are, wherever that may be, whatever our interior state of health. And we will know that we have met Him when we can say with the madman in today's Gospel: "What have I to do with thee, Jesus, Thou Son of God Most High?" When we can ask ourselves what is our true relationship with Christ.

We will know that *salvation* has reached us, however, when our answer to that question leads to change, to inner – and outward – change. May our meeting with Christ in this Liturgy be a moment when we ask this question, and may the change that God's grace makes possible take place in our lives and in our hearts. Amen.

10th November 1991

NO ESCAPE FROM INCARNATION

Luke 10: 25-37

There are just two verses I wish to draw to your attention in the Parable of the Good Samaritan, and they are the last in the passage which we have just heard read: having told the story of the priest, the Levite and the Samaritan, Jesus then asks the lawyer who had questioned him initially: "Which now of these three, thinkest thou, was neighbour unto him that fell among the thieves?" The lawyer answers correctly, as far as Jesus is concerned, when he says: "He that showed mercy on him."

Now what is interesting here is that the relationship of "neighbourliness" is not defined by what the Samaritan thinks, or what he feels – in fact we are told very little about this – but by what he does. He is a neighbour because he *behaves* like a neighbour, because he *acts* like a neighbour. It is what he *does* that matters. And what I wish to suggest this morning is, that this is a characteristic feature of Jesus' teaching: somehow *we* are what we *do*. Not that other aspects of our relationship with each other and with God are of no interest, but the "bottom line", as people now say, is action.

This is clear in today's parable. It is even more clear in Matthew 25, the parable of the Sheep and the

Goats. There the righteous do not even *know* that they are serving Christ when they care for the sick, give food and clothes to the poor, visit prisoners, provide shelter for strangers. But their *understanding* of what they are doing is not taken into account. It is enough that they do it.

A similar point is made in Matthew 11, when John the Baptist, who has been thrown into prison by Herod, sends two of his disciples to ask Christ if He is indeed "he that should come, or do we look for another?" Jesus says to them: "Go and show John those things which ye hear and see: the blind receive their sight, and the lame walk, the lepers are cleansed, and the deaf hear, the dead are raised up, and the poor have the gospel preached to them."

Now of course all these things are taking place in both the material *and* the spiritual realm, but it is to the concrete world of matter that Jesus draws John's attention: if things are happening there, then we can be sure that they are happening in the spiritual realm as well.

So, too, in a passage in Luke just before the one we heard this morning, the account of the sending of the seventy which is read for the feast of St Michael and all the angels and archangels: when the disciples return from their mission and report their success, Jesus replies: "Behold, I give unto you power to tread on serpents and scorpions, and over all the power of the enemy: and nothing shall by any means hurt you." Again, the primary reference is to the evil spirits, over which the disciples are to have control, but that invisible world is nevertheless firmly linked to the visible world of scorpions and serpents.

All this may seem simple, it may seem obvious. And yet it makes a very important point: in Christianity there is no escape from incarnation. God did not become man, did not take on flesh in order to provide us with a spiritual life. The Son of God did not become the Son of man in order to remove us from this world. God became one of us in order to integrate all levels of being, from the highest to the lowest, and to show us how to live on all these levels at once.

This is the point that Christ is making when he asks us to judge the three characters in today's parable by what they *do*. The love Christ shows us is an *incarnate* love, though its origin is deep in the Godhead. The love Christ asks of us is also an incarnate love, though it can only be a response to what comes down to us from heaven. In the language of St Paul, Christ has come to make the "inner" man and the "outer" man one. And to be his disciples, our faith must take on flesh as he did. Until what we believe, what we feel, what we think, has found expression *here*, in this material world, we have not become true followers of Christ. Amen

24th November 1991

THE SABBATH AND THE EIGHTH DAY

Luke 13: 10-17

We have heard this morning the story of the healing of a woman who had been crippled, bowed down and unable to lift herself up, for eighteen years. That Jesus should heal her is marvellous in itself, yet the Evangelist is actually more interested, to judge from the space he devoted to it, in the fact that this miracle took place on the Sabbath day, the day on which it was forbidden for anyone, including doctors and healers, to do any work. Unless, of course it was required to save someone's life.

Now this is not the only time that Jesus broke the Sabbath intentionally. The cripple by the pool of Bethesda was also healed on the Sabbath, as was the man with the withered hand. So was a man who was paralyzed, while on another Sabbath the eyes of a blind man were opened by Christ so that he could see. And then there was the incident when the disciples plucked ears of corn and ate them, something which it was not lawful to do on the Sabbath day. This Jesus justified by referring to the time when David and his companions had eaten the shewbread offered to God in the temple at a time when they were desperate for food.

All these passages suggest that something important is at stake here. And we can ask ourselves, what is it?

Perhaps the way to begin is with the Jewish Sabbath itself. Respect for the Sabbath is one of the most important features of Jewish popular piety and of the Mosaic law. Ultimate justification for this observance of a day of rest is found in the Genesis account of creation, where God rested from his labours on the seventh day. And in a Jewish community the quiet of the Sabbath rest meant that the presence of God, the nearness of God to his people, was particularly perceptible.

And suddenly, into this silence, into this presence, come Jesus' miracles. For some they are disturbing. They are contrary to the law. But Jesus suggests that these healings actually *belong* to the sabbath, and that even the rabbinic law somehow points in this direction. The Sabbath itself, by its nature, is open in the direction of healing and salvation.

For the Sabbath is not only a day when God rests and we rest, and when God is somehow more present to us than on other days. It is also a day when God acts. But when he acts it is to reveal the eighth day breaking in on the Sabbath day, the seventh day.

The healing and restoration that belongs to the eighth day, the day of the Kingdom, can be seen already on the Sabbath, as a foretaste of what is to come.

Now the point I wish to make is that the period through which we are living, which in Christian terms is the period between the Crucifixion of the Messiah and his Second Coming in glory, is itself a Sabbath day, the Sabbath day of history. The Crucifixion took place on Friday, the day of preparation, while Sunday, in the Church's calculation, is not only the first, but also the eighth day of the week, the day of the age to come, the day of Christ's coming again in glory. The Sabbath day of history corresponds to the whole of the period between these two events, to the whole of our present age until the end.

So let us take this Sabbath of history seriously. Let us first try to achieve that quiet which enables us to notice the presence of God. And then let us be open to the working of God in the midst of our rest, sensitive to the way in which the eighth day is already present in the seventh – in prayer, in the Liturgy, in communion, in our dealings with one another. And may our lives not be without these small miracles of healing which Christ has shown us *belong* to the Sabbath, and therefore to our lives *now*. Amen.

8th December 1991

TO GIVE IS TO RECEIVE

Luke 18: 18-27

Today's Parable of the Rich Young Man, which we heard in the reading from Luke, is appropriate to this period before Christmas in a number of ways, but I would like this morning to look at what one might call the "deep structure"of Jesus' reply to the Rich Young Man and apply it, if possible, to Christ Himself and to ourselves.

You will remember how Jesus, in reply to the question, "What shall I do to inherit eternal life?" replies, quite simply, "You know the commandments..." and then proceeds to list a few of the ten. But when the young man confesses to having kept these from his youth up, and obviously still wants something more, Jesus then continues: "Yet lackest thou one thing: sell all that thou hast, and distribute unto the poor, and thou shalt have treasure in heaven: and come, follow me."

Now this is a very important saying, and is already related to another "word" of Christ, also in Luke, in which he says: "When you have done all those things which are commanded you, say, 'We are unprofitable servants; we have done that which was our duty to do'" (Luke 17:10).

But what interests me in this saying is the sequence of events: divest yourself of all that you have, give to the poor, and then you will acquire treasure in heaven. For we can see here the pattern of the Incarnation, the pattern of God's activity for our salvation.

The Son of God, in order to become the Son of man, must also divest himself, in some sense, of what he has: the glory which was his from before the foundation of the world. He must give up that overwhelming power which is God's, and accept the powerlessness of man. He must sell what he has. And why? In order to make it available to the poor. So that what *He* has as God by nature, *we* may share by grace. In the language of the Fathers, "God became man, that man might become God."

And at one level Christ does all this to receive the same reward he promises to the Rich Young Man. As man, as incarnate man, the Son of God become the Son of man, Christ also lives in expectation of treasure in heaven. But to understand what this might mean we need to grasp three things.

The first is that the "promise of the Father" which Jesus instructs his disciples to wait for in Jerusalem, which we know to be gift of the Spirit, is not just a promise made to those who are his followers. It is a promise made by the Father to Jesus as well, who as Son of man must first receive this gift before he can pass it on to his disciples.

The second is that the Kingdom of heaven and the gift of the indwelling Spirit are one. The Spirit is the instrument of God's reign on earth, and without the gift of the spirit we cannot experience the Kingdom as a present reality *now*. If this is not clear from the Gospels as a whole – and it is – then we can point to an ancient variant reading in the Lord's Prayer, known and commented on by Maximus the Confessor, in which the petition, "Thy Kingdom come", is replaced by "the Holy Spirit come upon us and cleanse us."

Thirdly, we should realize that what Christ gives us, he has also received. In an important passage in Luke Jesus says to his disciples: "And I appoint unto you a kingdom, as my Father hath appointed unto me; that ye may eat and drink at my table in my Kingdom, and sit on thrones, judging the twelve tribes of Israel" (Luke 22:29-30). The word translated as "appoint" in the Authorized Version could easily be rendered as "assign" or "confer". The meaning is clear: Christ gives to his disciples what his Father has given him.

And, finally, perhaps we should remember that "heaven" is not just "up there" somewhere. It is *within* us as well: "the Kingdom of God", the Kingdom of heaven, "is within you."

Now when we take all these passages together we can see, I think, that the pattern which underlies Jesus' response to the Rich Young Man is in fact the same pattern that structures our salvation: God divests Himself in Christ of what is His by nature in order to give to us, the poor, what is His. Jesus, as the Son of man, receives in return the "promise of the Father", the Spirit, the same "treasure in heaven" which He promises to the Rich Young Man in today's Gospel. And finally, Christ shares this promised Spirit with His disciples – and us – at Pentecost. The Rich Young Man in the Gospel has already, in effect, been told to do this when he was told to give what he has to the poor.

There is one last point to be made. When Jesus has told the Rich Young Man that after he has given away what he has he will receive in return the Spirit, "treasure in heaven", he adds: "And come, follow me." Here we rejoin Christ's promise to his disciples of a kingdom, the Kingdom assigned to Him by His Father. Because before making this promise Jesus says to the Twelve, "Ye are they which have continued with me in my temptations."

In other words, the Twelve have followed Him in His trials as God put Him to the test. The Rich Young Man is *also* invited to join Christ where He is. We know, of course – as perhaps the young man did not know – that to be with Christ in this way is also a prerequisite for the gift of the Spirit. Only those who have stayed with Christ, who have lived His sufferings with Him, receive the promise of the Kingdom. So Christ tells the Rich Young Man that to enjoy this promised treasure, he must follow Him.

But this means, at the deepest level, that he must follow Christ – the Son of God become the Son of man – in the whole of his saving ministry. To divest ourselves of our wealth in order to share what we have with the poor. And to do so in expectation that God will in return bless us with the gift of the Spirit. And, if we truly follow Christ in all things, to give away that gift in turn, to share the Spirit with the poor. Only in this way will we be truly alive, truly living members of the Church, the Body of Christ, broken for many for the remission of sins and the salvation of the world. Amen.

15th December 1991

THE LIGHT OF THE WORLD

Mt. 4: 12-17

Today, on the Sunday after Theophany on the Old Calendar, we celebrate the beginning of Christ's public ministry, the ending of His years of silence and the commencement of the preaching of the coming of the Kingdom of God. It is seen by the author of today's Gospel passage as the coming of light, an increase in light, a great light rising up to shine on those in darkness. It is seen as illumination.

But if the coming of Christ, the preaching of Christ, is illumination, just what is it illumination of? In the Gospel passage itself, we are not told. Nor are we told specifically elsewhere in the Gospel. With a reticence that resembles that of Christ himself, the author of the narrative tells the story, and waits for us to come to our own conclusions as to what it is exactly that Christ's coming and his preaching cast light upon.

And he can do this because, if we think about it, it is clear – at least for those who have eyes to see – that the whole of Christ's life, everything He does or says, is a source of light illumining the mind and heart, the spiritual faculty in man which can "see" what is hidden from the eyes of the body and understand what is not comprehensible by the ordinary processes of discursive reason.

The passage that immediately follows today's reading describes the calling of the first Apostles, Andrew and Peter, James and John. It took just a word from Jesus and they "saw". They saw a new world opening up to them, a world of commitment to God in Jesus, one whom they would only gradually learn to be the Christ. They "saw", and their lives were changed.

Light also came to Zacchaeus, whose story we shall hear in two weeks' time. Only here it was his relationship to others that was changed. The light he saw in Christ was a call to justice, to evenhandedness in dealing with others, to sharing with the poor.

Light also came to the woman who washed Christ's feet with her tears in the house of Simon the Pharisee. She saw in Christ the forgiveness of God and the possibility of salvation. There is no indication that Jesus had ever spoken one word to her before. And yet she "saw"; she "saw" and was led to repentance.

Light also came to the disciples when, after the Crucifixion, they were finally able to see in Christ's death on the Cross a revelation of God's love and the possibility of newness of life and victory over death and the powers of darkness.

In all these ways Christ showed Himself to be the "light of the world". In each situation the true nature of God, the same face of God was revealed. This is marvellous, something wonderful in itself. But what I want to stress this morning is not this, but something which is in its own way greater. And this is that *we* are called to be light as well.

Christ tells His disciples – and *we* are His disciples – "You are the light of the world... Let your light so shine before men that they may see your good works, and glorify your Father which is in heaven." In these words is contained the whole thrust of the Incarnation: the Son of God becomes the Son of man that we may become by grace what He is by nature. And in this case, as He is light by nature, we are called by Him to become light by grace.

"As my Father hath sent me, so send I you." These words are spoken to us all. And as the Father sent His Son into the world to be the light of the world, so the Son sends us to be the light of the world.

There is no way of getting around this. Each one of us must ask himself whether he or she is in fact a disciple of Christ. And to be a disciple in the context of today's Gospel – and the whole of Christ's teaching – is to be a light, "a light to lighten the Gentiles", to be people in whose lives can be seen commitment to God, commitment to justice in our dealings with others and in the relations of peoples and nations. To be people who know how to forgive, because they themselves know forgiveness. To be people who know the power of the Cross, the revelation of God's strength in weakness, weakness voluntarily assumed so that others may be saved.

Let us remember, then, that we are called to be light. All that we have in Christ we have received freely as a gift. Let us give freely in return. The Orthodox faith is itself a light. Let us not put it under a bushel, but on a candlestick, that it may give light to all that are in the house. And may the light of our good works accompany the light of our faith, that the world may believe. Amen.

26th January 1992

WE ARE SAVED TOGETHER

Luke 18: 10-14

Today we begin our long journey through the services of the *Triodion* to Easter. And here, at the very beginning, we come upon the parable of the Publican and the Pharisee, placed here to remind us that whatever effort we may expend in keeping the Fast, ultimately it is contrition of the heart and openness to God that is the goal of all ascetic endeavour. Without this our efforts remain empty, unable to reunite us with our Creator.

But this morning I wish to look briefly at another aspect of today's reading, the words of the Pharisee himself: "God, I thank thee that I am not as other men are, extortioners, unjust, adulterous, or even as this publican." These words – and the thoughts which they express – are among the most destructive we can ever entertain. On one level they destroy our solidarity with one another, in that they deliberately introduce division in the body of the Church, in the worshipping and praying community. On another level, they destroy our unity with ourselves: for to the extent that we are blind to our own problems we can never hope to find that integration of mind and heart that enables the inner and outer man to be one. And finally, such thoughts destroy repentance, which is our only means of access to the Father.

And all this they do essentially because they are false: they are false when uttered by the Pharisee: they are false when we say them in one form or another to ourselves; they are false *whenever* they are used by *anyone*; they are false because we are in fact *like* each other, not *unlike*. The difficulties and temptations that *one* of us has we shall *all* have, sooner or later, in one form or another. For anyone to think that he or she is somehow different in this respect is a profound untruth, which can only have its origin in the "father of lies" himself.

We are each of us unique, irreducible in our personhood; but the temptations, the difficulties, we experience are the same, differing only in their intensity and in the way they combine themselves in our lives. No one of us can truly say: "I thank thee, O Lord, that I am not as other men." We *are* like each other. And to realise this is to make a start on the road to Easter. Because the purpose of the Fast, in which we share, and the purpose of Christ's Resurrection itself, is not that we should be saved individually, but that we should be saved *together*. That we should become one body, the Body of Christ, and enjoy corporately participation in His victory over death.

Let us put aside then the thought that we are unlike others, whether better or worse, and make our own the words of the Publican: "God be merciful to me a sinner." Amen.

16th February 1992

CHIEF AMONG SINNERS?

Matt. 6: 14-21

In the prayer before communion we hear these words: "I believe, Lord, and I confess, that thou art of a truth the Christ, the Son of the living God, who came into the world to save sinners of whom I am chief." We hear these words frequently, each Sunday, and it is right that we should do so, for they sum up succinctly our faith and our personal relationship with God. We should interiorize them, learn them by heart.

And yet, from time to time, people will come to me and say: "How can I make these words my own? I don't really *believe* that among all sinners I am *chief*. A sinner, yes, and a bad one. But not the worst of the lot." For such a person the requirement of *truth* seems to prevent them from making this prayer their own.

Today's reading from St Paul's Epistle to the Romans offers an answer to this question, and does so by means of a very simple image. St Paul says, to begin with: "Let not him that eateth despise him that eateth not; and let not him which eateth not judge him that eateth..." And then he adds: "Who art thou that judgeth another man's servant? To his own master he standeth or falleth." In other words, judgement belongs to our fellow Christian's master, to Christ, and not to us. The relationship of master and servant is not one into which we can enter, we cannot know it from within. And therefore, we cannot pass judgement on its true nature.

But if we turn aside from judging our brothers and sisters in the Church, there is just one relationship left where the judgement of God concerns us and where we can feel free to judge: our own relationship with Christ, our own relationship with the Saviour. We are "chief" among sinners because we are the "first". And when we judge ourselves, then, we are both "first" and "last", since there is no one else we can take into account.

St Paul, by the image he has chosen, encourages us to look upon ourselves as servants, servants of Christ, and therefore to apply to ourselves the words used in every weekday Vespers: "As the eyes of servants look unto the hands of their masters, as the eyes of the handmaiden look unto the hands of her mistress, so do our eyes wait upon the Lord our God."

To be a good servant is to be attentive, to be sensitive to the smallest sign, to be alert for the softest word. How can we have time to look at and judge others, if all our attention is directed towards Christ?

So let us today resolve not to judge one another. Instead, let us inwardly turn ourselves towards Christ. Let us clear our hearts and our minds of the background noise of judgement and criticism, so that we can hear what Christ has to say to us, and can find His hand guiding us in the most ordinary moments of our lives. Amen.

8th March 1992

OUR REST - GOD'S OPPORTUNITY TO ACT

Mark 8: 34-9:1

We are now entering the fourth week of Lent, and because the Great Fast is seven weeks long, this week lies right in the middle of our preparation for Easter, right at the very heart of the Fast. And throughout this week the icon of the Cross, presented to the faithful for their veneration, will lie in the middle of the church surrounded by flowers. It was last night, during the Vigil Service, that we placed the cross in this position. Earlier, before the Vigil had begun, the priest prepared for this by placing the icon of the Cross, and its decorated tray, on the side altar in the sanctuary, and then, in a short service, by himself, transferred it to the main altar. There, according to the tradition, for a short while it replaces the Gospel which normally lies at the centre of the altar. The Gospel book itself was made to stand upright, behind the cross.

Then, towards the end of the Vigil Service, after the singing of the Great Doxology, the icon of the Cross was carried out solemnly into the middle of the church for all to venerate. All this we know, and it is part of our experience of the worship of the Church. But Orthodox services are complex, and things are often done during them which pass unnoticed, even though symbolically they may be very important. It is one such detail that I would like to speak about this morning.

When the cross was placed in the centre of the altar and the gospel placed behind it, a decision had to be taken, because on the two covers of the gospel there are two different icons, one of the Crucifixion, the other of the Resurrection. Last night the gospel book was so placed that it was the icon of the Resurrection that could be seen. As a result, one looked *across* the Cross at the icon of the Resurrection, or to describe this in terms which reflect more adequately the *meaning* of what was done, one looked *through* the Cross *to* the Resurrection.

This detail from last night's service and its inner meaning confirms the significance of the whole week: by placing the Cross in the middle of the church as we come to the middle of our approach to Easter, we are not only reminded that the Cross is at the very centre of our faith, but are also reminded that we must pass *through* the Cross if we are to reach Christ's Resurrection.

But if on the altar there is a space, though a small one, between the icon of the Cross and the icon of the Resurrection, and if, in the unfolding of the Great Fast there is an interval between our veneration of the Cross at this service and our celebration of the Resurrection in four weeks time, so in history there was an interval between Christ's death and His Resurrection in the power and glory of God.

Liturgically, this is commemorated on Great Saturday, the day between Good Friday and Easter, and the liturgical texts for that day stress that Christ, having died, has *rested* from His labours. He has entered into His rest. As one of the hymns for Vespers of Great Saturday expresses it: "Suffering death in accordance with God's plan for our salvation, He kept the Sabbath in the flesh." "This is the blessed Sabbath, this is the day of rest, on which the only-begotten Son of God rested from all His works." On this day Christ rested and allowed his Father and the Holy Spirit to act.

Now what I *really* want to say – and this is *all* I really want to say – is that what Christ did, *we* must do also: we must rest from our works. Or better, we must rest from *our* works, so that God can act.

And yet what a paradoxical thing this is, since while we are still alive, we must continue to act. The change we are being asked to make must therefore be an *inner* change; and the rest into which we are asked to enter must be an inner rest. A change of heart. An acceptance that *our* works are nothing, while *God's* works *in* us are all.

St Paul speaks of this in Galatians when he says that "man is not justified by works of the law, but by faith in Jesus Christ." This is true because it is through faith that we enter into God's rest – which is also *our* rest – and into a new world in which what we do is *not* ours, but God's.

Christ entered into His rest through death, death on the Cross. But He also entered His rest through faith and *in* faith – faith and trust in the love and strength of His Father. We, too, can only enter our rest in faith, trusting that when we have died to our own strength, then the strength of God will find a place in us. Again, St Paul speaks of this when he says: "I am crucified with Christ: nevertheless I live; yet not I, but Christ liveth in me: and the life which I now live in the flesh I live by the faith of the Son of God, who loved me, and gave Himself for me."

The point at which St Paul is living when he talks like this is located, in time, between Good Friday and Easter, and, in space, between the icon of the Cross and the icon of the Resurrection.

The services of Lent, and more especially the services of Holy Week and Easter, enable us to live in this same time and space; to live in the realm of God's rest. Let us take this opportunity to experience in our hearts what this rest means, and to let *our* works cease and God's work begin. Amen.

29th March 1992

PREACHING THE GOSPEL TO ALL CREATION

Mark 15:14 - 16:20

Christ is Risen!

This Sunday, the Sunday of the Myrrh-bearing Women, is probably the only time during the Church's year that the Gospels read at Matins and the Liturgy are consecutive: the Matins Gospel in last night's Vigil follows on directly from the passage we have just heard and completes the final chapter of St Mark. So I shall take the liberty of preaching on last night's Gospel as if it were today's. On one verse in it, that is: the passage in which Christ, after the Resurrection, tells his disciples to "go into all the world, and preach the Gospel to every creature."

This is one of those hidden puzzles in the scriptures, hidden because we do not appreciate how strange it is. What can it mean to "preach the Gospel to every creature?" We normally think of preaching to *people*, to human beings who can understand what is being said. But "creature" is not a very specific word, and we often use it to refer to animals in general. In fact, if we look to the Greek text for help, we find that the difficulties are increased: the expression Mark has used is even more general, and means "creation". Christ, we are told here, has asked us, "to preach this Gospel to all creation". What *can* this possibly mean?

Before we answer this question we shall have to understand what is meant here by "the Gospel". The central message of Christ's preaching was His proclamation that "the kingdom of God is at hand". This is the "good news", the "Gospel" which He spreads among the people, inviting them to respond and prepare themselves to receive it. Later on the essential preaching of the disciples and Apostles was that the kingdom of God had now come "with power", ushered in by the death and Resurrection of Christ and made available to man through the descent of the Holy Spirit at Pentecost. Entry into that Kingdom, into that world of Christ's victory over death, was through baptism preceded by repentance.

But if preaching the Gospel means preaching the advent of the Kingdom, what is, in fact the Kingdom? Now what it is *not* is a geographical area like the "Kingdom of France" or the "Kingdom of Great Britain and Northern Ireland". Kingdom here means "kingship" or "rule", and the Kingdom of God exists anywhere that God is Lord, that God is King. It is not a thing, or a place, but a way of being related to God, and to be part of the Kingdom means to have undergone a qualitative change in one's mode of being. It means to live in the knowledge that God is King and Lord and to let that knowledge inform the whole of our lives; to let it begin in our hearts, then find a place in our minds, and finally be reflected in what we think, say and do. In other words, we do not enter the Kingdom, we do not live in the Kingdom, only through what we think or believe. The Kingdom of God has a claim on the whole of us, the whole of our being, and until the Kingdom of God has penetrated everything we do, we do not fully belong to it, we are not fully its members.

When we are fully members of the Kingdom, when the power of God is reflected in all that we think and say and do, then we shall be able to preach not just in words, but in deeds: our acts themselves will proclaim the nearness, the presence, the reality of the Kingdom. Even the things that we make with our hands will be an expression of God's Kingdom. And then, finally, the Kingdom of God will have penetrated through us, by means of our repentance and turning to God, into every level of creation.

We preach to the inanimate world through what we make of it. We preach to plants by the way we grow them, to animals by the way we treat them, to children by the way we raise them, to adults by the way we meet their spiritual, psychological and material needs. But we will be far from the truth if we think that this just means leading a good and moral life. Much more than this is involved. In some sense beauty is involved. And this is implied in Christ's words: "Go and preach the Gospel to all creation." For to bring the Kingdom of God into relationship with matter is to cause matter to reflect the glory of God, to become itself an outpost of the Kingdom.

Yet there is something paradoxical here, because the material world, as created by God, already reveals His glory. This is perhaps most powerfully expressed in the "Hymn of the Three Holy Children" which is sung during the Liturgy on Great Saturday. There all the elements of creation are called upon to "praise the Lord and exalt Him above all for ever": the angelic powers, the heavens, the sun and moon, light and darkness, day and night, the rain, the cold, the mountains, hills and seas, all fowls and beasts of the forest and the field, all the spirits of the living and the dead – all are called upon to praise the Lord. But of course they are doing this already, without being told to do so. All things, as created by God, praise Him through the way in which they reflect His glory. And so for us to preach the Gospel to every creature would appear to be to preach to the converted: the material world in its very createdness is turned toward God, points toward God, is a wordless word revealing God.

So we end up preaching the Kingdom only to those things that we touch, only to those parts of the material world we take for our own needs and purposes, only to those plants and animals whose existence we affect. Only to these can we personally bring the presence of God's Kingdom.

And what a responsibility this is. It means struggling not to export our fallenness into the rest of creation. To avoid creating ugliness by letting our hands, as we legitimately use the goodness of this world, create beauty instead. This is what it means to "preach the Gospel to every creature".

In these words of Christ therefore is to be found the heart of an Orthodox "ecology", for our task is not just to create a world in which man and other creatures can be at home, truly at home, but to create a world in which God can feel at home alongside us; a world in which our labours reflect the beauty of the Triune deity; a world in which even man's works give praise to God and "exalt Him above all for ever."

This cannot be done without a certain tenderness towards the world of matter. The Myrrh-bearing

Women whom we remember today can help us understand what this might mean. "Very early in the morning...at the rising of the sun", they brought "sweet spices, that they might come and anoint Him." That they might anoint Christ's body, that they might treat with reverence the material body of the immaterial God. In the tenderness and respect they showed towards matter, they were "preaching the Gospel to all creation". And they were able to do so because the love of Christ had filled the whole of their being.

Let us follow their example. And may *our* love of Christ, the Son of God become the Son of Man, lead us to reverence the material world which He created as a body for Himself, and may we be enabled thereby to bring the Gospel, the "good news" of the coming of God's Kingdom, to every creature and to all creation. Amen.

Christ is Risen!

10th May 1992

GIVEN OVER TO DEATH

2 Cor. 4: 6-15

The period of the Church's year in which we now find ourselves, the ten days between Ascension and Pentecost, is very interesting from a liturgical point of view. Nothing much is taking place. We have ceased singing "Christ is risen" and have not yet begun to sing "O heavenly King", the hymn to the Holy Spirit which we will only begin to use again next week at Pentecost. It is perhaps the "lowest" period of the year. We are waiting, as the Apostles once waited, for the "promise of the Father", for the gift of the Holy Spirit to the Church. It is a period characterised by absence. Christ is absent and the Spirit has not yet come. Even the figure of Christ is absent from the large crucifix here in the church: the empty Cross reminds us of the Resurrection, but we miss Christ's face. Only in and through the Spirit, however, can we see Christ, and so a certain darkness characterises this time.

As a result, the reading from 2 Corinthians which we heard this morning is particularly appropriate, for in it Paul, on his typically cosmic scale, draws a connection between the way God caused "the light to shine out of darkness" at the creation of the world, and the way His light has "shone in our hearts" – the darkness of our hearts – "to give the light of the knowledge of the glory of God in the face of Jesus Christ." There is probably a reference here to Paul's experience on the road to Damascus, when he saw Christ, whose followers he was persecuting, and heard Him speak to him. In both passages this light, this knowledge, is thought of as something which can be carried about within oneself, and so the recipient of this knowledge becomes a kind of "vessel". In Acts Christ tells Ananias that Paul is "a chosen vessel", while in 2 Corinthians Paul himself speaks of "earthen vessels", one adjective being used to highlight God's freedom in bestowing the gift of understanding, the other to point out our own unworthiness.

Paul then goes on to speak about the condition of those who have received this gift, again based upon his own experience. And it is a most important vision: "We are constantly bearing about in our bodies the dying of the Lord Jesus, that the life also of Jesus might be made manifest in our bodies." That light of which he speaks is the light of the Risen Christ, the light he saw when Christ appeared to him on the road to Damascus. And this is not just an inner light, but a light which is to be manifest in our bodies, the uncreated glory of God made visible in the world. The light of the Resurrection will not work in us only at some time in the future, but is present in us now, in these "earthen vessels" which need to be completely renewed.

It is typical of Paul that he brings all of this into relationship with the Crucifixion. God has drawn near us through death. Now *we* are given a chance to draw near to God through death. Yet in the midst of death there is life, and in the midst of darkness, light. "We are troubled on every side, yet not distressed; we are perplexed, but not in despair; persecuted, but not forsaken; cast down, but not destroyed. Always bearing about in the body the dying of the Lord Jesus, that the life also of Jesus might be made manifest in our bodies." The approach to life, eternal life, is the same both for us and for Christ, both for man and for the God-man. A single path lies open before us, a path along which Christ has walked, a path along which we, too, are invited to walk.

What is needed is discernment. We need to be able to recognise what it is in all that happens to us that offers us a way toward God. What it is that will make it clear that the victory belongs to God and not to us. That the life we live comes not from below but from above. Paul makes this clear: those who truly live – live, that is with the eternal life of God – are constantly being delivered to death, handed over to death. And this takes place so that the immortal life of Christ may be made manifest in their mortal bodies.

This was true of the Apostles. It is true of us. God does not seem to have another way of bringing us into relationship with himself at the depth of communion which he seeks. We may not find this comfortable – why should we? – but we can rejoice in it none the less. "For," in the words of St Paul which follow directly on from the passage we heard this morning, "though our outward man perish, yet the inward man is renewed day by day. For our light affliction, which is but for a moment, worketh for us a far more exceeding and eternal weight of glory; while we look not at the things which are seen, but at the things which are not seen: for the things which are seen are temporal; but the things which are not seen are eternal."

Let us bear these words of St Paul in mind when we look at our own lives. And may we remember that it is by being "given over to death" that our feet are placed firmly on the path to eternal life. Amen.

7th June 1992

THE POWER TO BIND AND TO LOOSE

Matt. 16: 13-19

Today we celebrate the feast of St Peter and St Paul. The gospel read for the feast specifically concerns St Peter, and in particular the gift given to him by Christ of the power to "bind and loose". The power to "bind and loose" is the power to forgive or not to forgive sins, an extraordinary power, and one which in traditional Jewish theology, as reflected in the New Testament, belongs exclusively to God. What Christ gives to Peter here is in fact something divine, called by Christ in fact "the key to the Kingdom of heaven", and rightly so, for entry into the Kingdom is possible only through reconciliation with God, and all reconciliation inevitably entails forgiveness.

But what we do not always remember is that the power to forgive sins is given by Christ not just once in the New Testament, but *three* times. It is given once specifically to Peter, and twice more generally to the disciples as a whole. The best known of these passages is found in John, where after the Resurrection – in fact, on that first Sunday evening after the women disciples found the empty tomb – Christ came to "where the disciples were assembled for fear of the Jews", and after He had blessed them with his peace, "he breathed on them" and said to

"Receive ye the Holy Ghost: Whosesoever sins ye remit, they are remitted unto them; and whosesoever sins ye retain, they are retained." We do not know how many disciples were present when Jesus appeared to them, but the implication is that it was the whole of the faithful community. We are only told that Thomas was not there when this happened.

The second instance of Christ's giving to the disciples in general the power "to bind and to loose" occurs in Matthew not long after He has given the same power to Peter. In the midst of a passage in chapter 18, where Christ is answering questions from the disciples, and specifically when He is dealing with trespasses within the community, He says: "Verily I say unto you, 'Whatsoever ye shall bind on earth shall be bound in heaven; and whatsoever ye shall loose on earth shall be loosed in heaven.'" Here again, the gift is to all the disciples, apparently without exception.

Now what this means with regards to Peter is quite clear: Peter exercises the power to bind and to loose within a community which, *as a whole*, has been given the power to bind and to loose. The power to forgive sins belongs to the *whole* of the Body of Christ. Peter's authority, which is real, is exercised not over against the community but within the community of which he is a member. And as if to emphasise the shared nature of the power to forgive sins, Christ, in this same passage from Matthew 18, goes on to say: "Again I say unto you, that if two or three of you shall agree on earth as touching anything they shall ask, it shall be done for them of my Father which is in heaven. For where two or three are gathered together in my name, there am I in the midst of them." When you realise that the original form of absolution in the Church was deprecative in character, that is, did not use the expression "I forgive" but rather called upon *God* to forgive the sinner, it would appear that Christ is quite clearly saying here that the forgiveness of sins is ultimately an act of the community, no matter how it may be articulated.

But just as important, to my mind, as this saying of Christ which brings out the communal nature of forgiveness, is the saying which immediately precedes the gift of the Holy Spirit and the power to forgive sins in John. There Christ says, again after blessing the disciples with His power: "As my Father hath sent me, so send I you." And at once He breathes on them and speaks to them about the forgiveness of sins. Here, too, the implication is clear: as Christ was sent to mediate the Father's forgiveness among men, so *we* are sent, as Christ's disciples, to mediate forgiveness as well.

When we say that the Church is "apostolic" we mean that it is *sent*, sent as the Apostles were sent and with the teaching and mission with which the Apostles were sent. *They* were sent to bring reconciliation with God to all mankind through forgiveness. And our task, too, as part of this Apostolic Church is to bring reconciliation with the Father to those around us, to mediate to them God's forgiveness.

But to do so effectively, we shall first have to forgive each other, we shall have to be reconciled with one another. No better image, no better icon of reconciliation could be given us than this feast of St Peter and St Paul. They were two very different people, with two very different calls from God, and yet were able to find in Christ a oneness, a unity of mind and heart which gave strength and power to their proclamation of the Gospel. Through their prayers may we, today, find the strength and inspiration to build up in our times the oneness and the unity of the Church. Amen.

12th July 1992

TO FORGIVE IS TO RECEIVE

Matthew 18: 23-35

The Gospel reading this morning takes the form of a parable, the parable about the king who wished to settle accounts with his servants. As such it is basically a story about something ordinary, but at the same time it speaks to us in a very deep way about the Kingdom of God.

Peter had come up to Christ and had asked him: "How often shall my brother sin against me, and I forgive him? Till seven times?" And Jesus replied: "I say not unto thee until seven times, but until seventy times seven." And then the parable follows in order to show how things work in the realm of forgiveness, which is the realm of the Kingdom.

There are many interesting things to be said about this parable, many questions which it raises, but what I wish to stress this morning is the discrepancy between what the wicked servant asks for and what he receives. When he is told by the king to repay the ten thousand talents which he owes – an immense sum – the servant begs for time to repay: "Lord have patience with me, and I will repay thee all." Yet the king does not say: "Very well then, I will give you another six months or a year in which to repay your debt." This in itself would have been enough to show his compassion. But instead, he releases his servant and forgives him his debt, cancelling it completely. The king now never expects to be repaid: the account has been settled: and the servant no longer owes him anything.

Of course, this tells us something about the king: he is a truly splendid ruler, so rich that he can afford to forgo an immense fortune and not feel threatened by the loss. And it also tells us something about his generosity, his willingness to give of what he has. But it tells us even more about his relationship to the servant, and therefore about God's relationship with us.

When appealing to the king the servant asks only for time. In other words, he fully acknowledges the debt. He does not question the amount. He does not ask to be released from his obligation. In fact, to do so would be to suggest that the king was in some way obliged to him, or that the debt was not what it seemed to be.

And this seems to me to say something not only about forgiveness, but about confession. What God asks of us in confession is not that we should negotiate with him, but simply that we should acknowledge the existence of the debt, and then be ready to do something about it. In the parable this takes the form of a willingness to repay in full. In confession it takes the form of a firm resolve to turn from our sins and to put things right as well. To receive the grace of forgiveness we do not need to ask for it. It is enough to acknowledge our debt. In fact, asking for forgiveness may even get in the way of that clarity of mind and heart which is one of the primary goals of our practice of confession.

But the most striking thing about this parable is what it says about forgiveness as grace, as gift, as something whose origin is God. As is always the case with the gifts of God, they are offered abundantly, but we are not always able to receive them. What today's parable says is clear: If we do not forgive those who have sinned against us, we cannot ourselves receive the forgiveness of God.

Our own lack of forgiveness blocks the path of God's grace. To receive the grace of forgiveness we must first forgive. In the ordinary world we give from what we have received, but in the world of forgiveness, we give in order to receive.

Now the spiritual life is about making new beginnings. And in two days' time, on 1st September we begin a new Church year. Let us take advantage of this moment to look at our relationships with one another and to ask ourselves: whom have I not forgiven? For having done this – and acted upon it – we will then be in a position to place ourselves with confidence before God, confessing our sins, and knowing that we have put nothing in the way of God's grace and forgiveness. Amen.

30th August 1992

IN THE SHIP WITH CHRIST

Luke 5: 1-11

The Gospel passage which we heard this morning, the final part of the 5th chapter of Luke, describes the circumstances of the calling of Peter, James and John, and it is their calling that I would like to comment on this morning. Unfortunately, however, it does not tell the whole story, since the story has already begun, so far as James and John are concerned, in Chapter 4. There, after healing a man possessed by an unclean spirit, Jesus enters the house of Simon Peter only to find his mother-in-law ill with a great fever. They beg him to do something for her, and he does: he "rebukes" the fever (to use the language of the Authorised Version) and it leaves her. And she gets up and resumes her normal household tasks. Jesus then proceeds to heal more people who are brought to him, and to cast out more demons.

It was only after all this had taken place that Jesus, because of the crowds, went out in Peter's boat into the lake of Gennesaret and preached from there to the people on the shore, speaking to those who wished to hear the word of God. And it was *after* he had finished teaching, that Jesus told Simon to let down his nets, and the resulting draft of fish convinced him that he should follow Christ.

What we see here are two levels of understanding combined in a third. To begin with, Peter sees the power of God in Christ's bringing his mother back to health. We ought not to think of this as something unusual in that day: there would have been many itinerant healers claiming to do – and doing – the same kind of thing. But Peter sees this personally in his own family. And he believes. He believes that God is working with and in Jesus.

Then Peter hears Jesus preaching the word of God. We know the content of that preaching, not from Luke so much as from Mark: Jesus proclaimed the Kingdom of God, declaring that the Kingdom of God was at hand, near at hand, and that it would soon come with power. From the fact that Peter stayed with Jesus, and lent him his boat to use, we can conclude that he accepted Christ's teaching. We may assume that he, too, looked for the coming of the Kingdom.

And then, in the great draft of fishes, he sees these two combined: the outward manifestation combined with the inner teaching. He sees the teaching of Christ reflected in the real world, expressed dramatically in the world of his own experience, and he believes, believes at such a depth and with such conviction that he can leave everything and follow Christ. And it is not because of the great catch of fish in itself that he leaves everything to follow Christ, but because Christ takes him even further when he says to him, quite simply: "From henceforth thou shalt catch men."

At that point Simon realised that the miraculous catch of fishes was not a "thing in itself", that it was not something solid, concrete, but that somehow it opened out onto eternity, onto the Kingdom. He understood that it was an invitation to join God in working for the salvation of men. He saw that the ship on which Jesus sat to teach – and in which *he* sat as well – was an image, an icon of the faithful community of the last days, what we would call the Church, and that he was being asked by God – through Christ – to help fill it, to add to the number of those who were being saved.

Brothers and sisters, we all, by the grace of God, are sitting in that ship with Christ. We are there because we have been caught up in the nets which the Apostles – and their successors – at Christ's command have cast over the world. But do we respond to this knowledge the way that Peter responded when he saw that he was himself, physically, in that ship with Christ, and that he was being asked to find others to join him there?

Apostleship in the Church does not belong just to the twelve, or to the seventy. It is a characteristic of the *whole* church. And until we have each one of us taken this in, made it part of our self-understanding as Christians, we will not have "heard" today's Gospel. May we all come to realise that the blessing of our presence in the Church, the blessing of being here in this ship with Christ, is ours only because we are among the fish whom the Apostolic Church has caught in its net. And may we come to realise that we are all called to be apostles, "fishers of men", as well. Amen.

11th October 1992

PERFECT AS GOD IS PERFECT

Luke 6: 31-36

When we listen to today's Gospel read in church, as we hear Christ speak to his disciples, we are faced once again by the *radicalism* and the *maximalism* of the Gospel. Yes, Christ preaches that the Kingdom of God is at hand, that the power of God which will finally fulfil all things is at work now in this world. That it is like a grain of mustard seed which will one day be a large plant, or like leaven, which from a small beginning works quietly and gently to leaven the whole mass of dough. But the fact that the Kingdom, its presence, is a hidden presence does not mean that those who know of its presence and in some sense already live at the end of time are permitted to "take life easy", to relax while they wait for God to act.

On the contrary, because they know the power of the Kingdom, because they already know its presence in the world, they are called by Christ to live as if God were already victorious, as if they themselves lived in the last days, as if, in a sense, history had already come to an end and that the calculations that ordinarily accompany all that we do were no longer necessary. They are asked to live their lives as if the future belonged entirely to God.

What is it if we love those who already love us? If we love those whose love we can count on in return? Even sinners, even those who are completely bound up with this world, will do the same. It is in fact quite rational to do so. What is it if we do good to those who have done good to us? Quite understandably even sinners will do the same, because they understand very well how to enter into the "give and take" that makes this world what it is. What is it if we lend – or put our money on deposit – where we can be sure of a good return? Sinners understand very well how these things work and make good use of them to their own ends.

No, all these things are human – and no doubt will never be eliminated from our lives while this world is still in existence. But the preaching of Christ is not that we should become human (though we should try this for a start), but that ultimately, in some sense, we are called to be divine. "Be ye merciful," he says, "as your Father is merciful." Or, in the words of the parallel passage in Matthew: "Be ye therefore perfect, even as your Father which is in heaven is perfect."

And what does it mean to be merciful as God is merciful, to be perfect as God is perfect? It is to love those who do not love you. It is to do good to those who have not done good to you. It is to give where you can have no expectation of gain. To do this, Christ says, is to be like the Father. To do this, he might have said, is to be divine. For God is kind even to those who are thankless, even to those from whom he cannot expect thankfulness in return. As Matthew tells us: "He maketh his sun to rise on the evil and on the good, and sendeth rain on the just and on the unjust."

Now what I want to suggest this morning is that God acts this way – *can* act this way – only because he is truly free, and that he is asking us, through Christ, to be truly free as well. To give when we have already received, to lend where we can expect to gain, to love where we are already loved – all this is to react to the world around us. It is to let ourselves be conditioned, determined, in a sense, by the circumstances of our existence. But to act where the circumstances do not rationally call for action and where no return can be expected is to act freely, from within.

May we all come to know this freedom, a freedom which Christ understands as the freedom to be merciful, knowing that this freedom and the mercy that goes with it are ultimately God's. In us they exist as gift. Christ took on flesh and became one with us in order to share with us this gift, and to enable us to become one with him and thereby children of one Father. And may we, as children of one Father, be merciful first to one another and then to those around us in the world. Amen.

17th October 1992

"HE SET HIS FACE TO GO TO JERUSALEM"

Luke 9: 51

This morning I wish to speak not about the two gospels that have been read, or the epistles, one each of the day and of the Saint, but of one verse in the Gospel of Luke that we actually read in the normal course of the Old Calendar readings on Thursday of this past week. The verse is Luke 9:51, and in we are told: "And it came to pass, when the time was come that Jesus should be received up, he steadfastly set his face to go to Jerusalem."

This is one of those "Johannine" passages in Luke where somehow for a moment the Evangelist steps back and looks *not* at the detail of what is happening but at the development of Christ's life as a whole. "To be received up" – or more accurately, "to be taken up" – refers here to the whole of Christ's movement toward the Father: the Cross, the Resurrection on the Third Day, the Ascension, and then finally the Sitting at the Right Hand in glory. All are part of a single movement upwards.

But what struck me was not this picture, but the expression, "he set his face to go to Jerusalem". The Greek says that he set it "firmly", while in the Authorised Version, we read "steadfastly". Christ turned his face towards the hills of Jerusalem, and climbed upwards towards the Cross.

Now this seems to me to say something very important about the Cross in our lives. We are accustomed to experiencing the difficulties of our lives as something of a cross, as a burden, difficult to bear, as something we can ask God to help us carry. From this point of view our cross appears as something either past or present, and more generally, as a reality over which we have no control. It is given to us, dropped on us by the conditions and circumstances of our lives. But when Jesus sets His face towards Jerusalem, the Cross He faces is before Him, it belongs to the future, it has not yet come upon Him. It belongs to the Father's future plan for Him, and not to the present or past circumstances of His life.

What a great difference there is here between this attitude of Christ and ours. For Christ the Cross is something which must be discovered, a path, a way which must be found, a call to self-transcendence, an approach to God. It is not something which is or has been.

For each of us God provides such a cross through which we can move out of ourselves towards Him. May the gift of communion with God which we find in the Eucharist enable us to discover this cross. For it is by taking up *this* cross that the other burdens of our lives are made light. Amen

8th November 1992

GOOD WORKS IN A NEW CREATION

Eph. 2: 4-10

Two weeks ago I spoke of the Cross as something which comes to us from the future, not a burden which we carry with us from the past, but a path opening out in front of us and leading to eternal life. In today's reading from St Paul's Epistle to the Ephesians a similar message is conveyed, though St Paul is not here speaking about the Cross, but about "works", and more specifically about "good works".

Paul begins by talking about salvation as a gift: we have been saved "by grace", raised up with Christ and made to sit with him in the heavenly places. Even this has been done only so that "in the coming ages God might show the immeasurable riches of his grace in kindness towards us in Christ Jesus". "For by grace you have been saved," he says "and this is not of your own doing, but a gift of God." We are not saved because of works, in other words, but by the freely given grace of God. In the fact that we have been saved there is nothing *we* can boast about, there is nothing we have *done*. We have simply been the recipient of God's gift.

Up to this point Paul has been speaking of salvation almost as if it were something external to ourselves. But now the language changes. We are, he says, "God's workmanship". We have been "created in Christ Jesus" – and since this is the second time that we have been created, he could just as well have said "recreated", we have become a "new creature" as he *does* say elsewhere. We have been made "alive together with Christ Jesus" in baptism through our sharing in the death and Resurrection of Christ.

And here St Paul comes to the purpose of all this: we have been recreated in Christ "for good works". Those very works, one might say, that could not save us in the first place now re-enter the picture. And what is more, they return as good works "purposed for us beforehand, that we should walk in them".

St Paul tells us here that for the person who has realised in his life the transforming power of baptism, who has been reborn, who has become a "new creation", there opens out a path which has been prepared for him by God. It is as if "the way that we should walk in" *approaches* us from the future, from the world to come. It enters the present from eternity.

We do not have to hunt for good works to do: God will provide. But we will only *see* what he has provided if we have been created anew.

So it is not just the Cross that stands in front of us, waiting for us to enter into it, to "take it up". The path of good works opens out in front of us as well. Both have been prepared for us by God. Both come to us from eternity, and are a revelation of God's eternal will for us. Together they delineate the path that leads us to salvation.

May God grant us the eyes to see both the good works he has prepared for us to walk in, and the Cross that lies before us as well. And may we not be surprised if the one is somehow bound up with the other. Amen.

22nd November 1992

LOOSING THE BONDS OF SATAN

Luke 13: 10-17

Throughout the Gospels – and throughout the activity and teaching of Christ – there is a constant dialectic between the inner and the outer, between what happens in the soul and what happens in the body, between what happens in individual people and what happens in society as a whole. And this is true of today's Gospel as well, which tells the story of the healing of the crippled woman on the Sabbath day.

Ostensibly what takes place in her takes place in her body: whereas before she could not stand, now she *can* stand. The power of God, working in Jesus, restores her outwardly to that image of God in which she was created. Yet this is not the only aspect of the image that is in play. There is another resonance here, which can be heard in the words Christ uses to address the hostile crowd: "Ought not this woman, being a daughter of Abraham (in other words, a daughter of faith), whom Satan hath bound, lo, these eighteen years, be loosed from this bond on the Sabbath day?" For the disciples of Christ who surrounded him – and if not for them, then at least for the Church after Pentecost – these words "to bind" and "to loose" would have echoed Jesus' words about the forgiveness of sins, and would have suggested to them that the work Christ came to do on the seventh day concerned not just the outer man, but the inner man as well. Not just the restoration of the outer image, but of the inner image also.

It is the restoration of the image of God that justifies the reading of the passage in the weeks before the Nativity of Christ. In the understanding of the Church, "God became man that man might become god." That he might be "divinised", that he might enter fully – or at least as fully as is possible for a created being – into the life of God. That he might be so transfigured by God's presence in him as to become immortal in both body, soul and spirit.

But does this process, which clearly takes place within the context of an individual life, have no social dimension? In broader terms, does the Nativity of Christ, which opens the way to deification for individuals, say nothing about our social life, and about our life together? From the point of view of Christian doctrine, it does say something about society, but within certain limitations.

In a sense we are asking the question, "What can be done to improve the quality of human life?" And there are, in fact, only three replies that have been given. The first is that the life of the individual can indeed be improved, by changing the *conditions* under which he or she lives. Improved conditions lead to a better, fuller, more human life. The second reply is that *education* is what is required: if people were only *told* what they needed to do in order to fulfil their true calling, they would do it. And the third reply, which is given perhaps its finest literary expression in the works of Dostoyevsky, is that even if society were perfect and every individual were shown clearly what he or she should do to be saved, to reach fullness of life, human beings would still be capable of choosing destruction, of turning away from God, of turning away from the divine life which is being offered them.

From this third point of view – which takes into account the Fall – when we have acted to improve society, raised the level of education, when we have given to charity to help save people from starvation or from the bestiality of war, everything still remains to be done. The process of divinisation, which is the promise of Christ's Nativity, has yet to begin.

And yet how necessary it is to work and give for the relief of hunger and the alleviation of the results of war. Because even if what is outside us does not *determine* what goes on within, does not *determine* our relationship to our own deepest vocation, nevertheless, it does influence it deeply. By changing the conditions of a person's outward existence we may at least make it *easier* for them to find the path to salvation and eternal life.

The struggle between God and Satan, which is the theme of today's Gospel, takes place not only in the outer world of the body and society, but in the heart of each one of us as well. The bonds of Satan can be seen quite clearly in the society in which we live, the bonds of greed and self-interest that seem to determine so much of what we do. Yet until we have found these same bonds at work in our own hearts, and have learnt to deal with them by God's grace, we shall hardly be able to deal with them adequately in the world at large.

So as we give – and give generously – this Christmas, let us remember that it is not just charity that begins at home, but that the greatest gift of all, the gift of salvation in Christ, must first be received before it can be shared, received within our hearts. And that when we have given to relieve suffering and need, the great work which God calls us to do has scarcely begun. Amen.

13th December 1992

ETERNITY - "GOD WITH US"

Matt. 1: 1-25

In the Gospel this morning we have heard not only the long genealogy of Christ – three times fourteen generations from Abraham, the first to hold the faith of Israel, through to Joseph the Betrothed, the seeming father on earth of our Lord and Saviour Jesus Christ – but we have also heard one of the many prophecies from the Old Testament that look forward to the coming Messiah, the Saviour of Israel, the Saviour of the world.

This prophecy is found in Isaiah, and reads in the Authorised Version: "Behold, a virgin shall be with child, and shall bring forth a son, and they shall call his name Emmanuel, which being interpreted is 'God with us'." I do not wish this morning to go into the well known scholarly discussion of whether the term "virgin", whose equivalent is also found in the ancient Greek translation of the Scriptures which is used in the Orthodox Church, is an appropriate rendering of the Hebrew text. I am more interested in the second half of the verse, which gives to this special child the name "God with us", "Emmanuel".

Now this expression, this name, when taken seriously, is even more astonishing than what is revealed in the first part of the verse, for the notion that God might be "with us" in a child is certainly, within the context of Judaism, even more of an affront to human understanding than the notion that a virgin should conceive. For, when taken as the Church has taken them, these words do not mean that in Jesus God is with us in some moral or ethical sense, as if He were "an outsider", agreeing with us in some comfortable manner, approving of what we think and do; they mean that He is *with us* in the sense of being present with us, dwelling among us bodily in that child, the incarnate Lord, "whom", in the words of the first Epistle of St John, who speaks here as an Apostle, "we have heard, whom we have seen with our own eyes, whom we have looked upon and our own hands have handled."

"God is with us" in the child Jesus; God is within the central mystery of the Church, the Eucharist; in Christ's own words, "I am with you always, even unto the end of the world." For having once become incarnate, God *will* not, in some sense *cannot*, abandon the world.

All that we do in the Church, all that we do as Christians should reflect this basic truth. The architecture of the Church should not suggest that God is "up there" somewhere, but that He is *here*, with us, as is done by the domes of Eastern churches, and even by the tent-like shape of our own. The epiclesis, that invocation of the Spirit upon the holy gifts during the Liturgy, is a prayer for the *descent* of the Holy Spirit: God comes *down* to us, to where we are; the Spirit joins us here where we are in order to transform the gifts – and us – into what we should be, here and now.

And, finally, the saints themselves, in whom Christ lives, are experienced by the Church as "God with us". In the person of the saint, God has visited His people. The blessing of the saint is the blessing of God. In the face of the saint we see that God is not "out there" but *here*, among His people.

So let us not forget the deep meaning of the name "Emmanuel". May we learn to see it realized in the mysteries of the Church; may we come to know its truth in the context of our lives. May we also learn to find it reflected, even if only dimly and often in distorted form, in the preparations for Christmas we see being made in the world around us. For in the generalized perception that this world *can* be a blessing, that the good things of this life have at least the potential to mean much more than they normally do, we have a dim, attenuated expression of that great truth that was proclaimed by the prophet long ago: the virgin's child is "God with us", "Emmanuel".